OPEN OUR EYES, OPEN OUR HEARTS

OPEN OUR EYES, OPEN OUR HEARTS

SEEING GOD IN EVERYDAY MOMENTS

MAIDA CARSON

XULON PRESS

Xulon Press
2301 Lucien Way #415
Maitland, FL 32751
407.339.4217
www.xulonpress.com

© 2023 by Maida Carson

All rights reserved solely by the author. The author guarantees all contents are original and do not infringe upon the legal rights of any other person or work. No part of this book may be reproduced in any form without the permission of the author.

Due to the changing nature of the Internet, if there are any web addresses, links, or URLs included in this manuscript, these may have been altered and may no longer be accessible. The views and opinions shared in this book belong solely to the author and do not necessarily reflect those of the publisher. The publisher therefore disclaims responsibility for the views or opinions expressed within the work.

Unless otherwise indicated, Scripture quotations taken from the King James Version (KJV) – *public domain.*

Scripture quotations taken from the New Century Version (NCV). Copyright © 2005 by Thomas Nelson, Inc. Used by permission. All rights reserved.

Paperback ISBN-13: 978-1-66287-829-9
Ebook ISBN-13: 978-1-66287-830-5

Table of Contents

Introduction 1
Do You Have Your Helmet On? 2
Be Quiet and Know 4
The Treasure Hunt 6
The Destroyer and the Savior .8
Making Taffy 10
Friends 12
Heroes 14
Another Place, Another Time 16
Peace and Quiet 18
Mending 20
What's in Your Hands? 22
Can You Hear It? 24
Pictures 26
Father's Love 28
Apples and Understanding 30
The Gift of Color 32
Are You Still In? 34
He'll Keep You Afloat 36
Mulberry Trees—What Do They Say to You? 38
Gift Baskets 40
Play Dough 42
Laughter 44
Encouragers 46

Children and Eagles	48
Grandma Maida's Scrapbook	50
A Daddy's Love	64
What's Goin' On?!	66
"You Never Know!"	68
The Real Princess Dress	70
What Do You See?	72
What Did You Learn in Sunday School?	74
Miss Emilee	76
Rainbows	78
The Good Shepherd	80
Bubbles, Sidewalk Chalk, and Love	82
Sowing Seeds	84
Ready, Set, Go!	86
Words	88
He's Watching You	90
Brotherly Love	92
Mama	94
Clean Windows	98
Princesses	100
Sunsets	102
Our Great Big Protector	104
Prayer Warriors	106
The Control Button	108
He Took His Flight Also	110
Who do you Prefer?	112
Life Giving Water	114
Leftovers	116
Acknowledgements	118

Introduction

While Jesus walked on this earth, He often taught in parables by using common circumstances to teach a spiritual lesson. He knew people had eyes to see and hearts to fill.

God has taught me much through the pure innocence of my young grandchildren. I invite you to come along with me on my life's journey and allow Him to teach you through ordinary, everyday circumstances. Watch as He lets us catch glimpses of who He is—His love, grace, mercy, power, strength, and compassion.

Soon you'll be seeing His touch all around you. Just open your eyes and open your heart.

Do You Have Your Helmet On?

"Accept God's salvation as your helmet, and take the sword of the Spirit, which is the word of God." Ephesians 6:1 (NCV)

"Brothers and sisters, think about the things that are good and worthy of praise. Think about the things that are true and honorable and right and pure and beautiful and respected. Do what you learned and received from me, what I told you, and what you saw me do. And the God who gives peace will be with you." Philippians 4:8-9 (NCV)

"Do not change yourselves to be like the world but be changed within by a new way of thinking. Then you will be able to decide what God wants for you; you will know what is good and pleasing to him and what is perfect." Romans 12:2(NCV)

Helmets are good, protective gear, even though they can be a little restrictive and uncomfortable at times. Nonetheless, they are imperative for safety. Four-year-old twins, Rayne and Carson, tried their best to get out of wearing them as they jumped on their bikes, ready to "hit the road" at the end of their cul-de-sac. Grandma heard everything from "They're too hot!" and "I can't snap it!"

to "Daddy says we don't have to wear them anymore cause we're good bike-riders!" Grandma still made them put their helmets on. Rayne's "wipe-out" the next week made believers out of them both. She only received scrapes on her hands and knees as her little body met the hard pavement. The helmet took the blow instead of her little head. They were two thankful children—thankful that Mommy and Daddy (and Grandma) loved them enough to keep them safe.

Have you put your helmet on yet? Have you accepted God's salvation? He came to give life—a rich, full life here on earth—and life forever with Him in Heaven. The same way that Rayne's helmet protected her from harm, God protects his children by aligning their thinking to His own. In Philippians, He tells us to think about the "good" things we see, hear, and know. The outcome is knowing He is with us, and that He brings peace to our hearts and minds. In Romans, He says this new way of thinking will help us know what to follow and what to stay away from—how to think the right way. Throughout the entire Bible, He tells us what is best for us.

The best—isn't that what your mama and daddy wanted for you? Isn't that what you want for your children? That's what our heavenly Daddy wants for us. Now, it's up to us to gear up! Have you got your helmet on? Don't leave home without it!

Be Quiet and Know

"God says, 'Be quiet and know that I am God. I will be supreme over all the nations. I will be supreme in the earth.'" Psalm 46:10 (NCV)

Butterflies are one of my favorite gifts of beauty from our Creator. So, when I saw a beautiful monarch sitting on the bright orange butterfly plant, I wanted my two-year-old grandson to enjoy it as well. For me, it always adds enjoyment to any moment when it's shared with someone special—especially a grandchild. I quietly said, "Wyatt, come over here slowly, be quiet and stand really still so we can watch him." Wyatt spied the butterfly and started to reach for him. I said, "You might scare him away." No sooner were the words out of my mouth than the butterfly hopped onto Wyatt's precious little finger. The butterfly just stayed there, content to rest on my two-year-old grandson's finger. It seemed like time stood still as Wyatt and I drank in the beauty of God's creation.

Have you done that lately? Have you taken the time to be quiet and just drink in the beauty of God's creation? A beautiful pink rose in full bloom. Delicate yellow and white honeysuckle blossoms—and, oh, the nearly intoxicating fragrance! A tiny hummingbird as he drinks the nectar from a bright red geranium. The falling autumn leaves creating a golden carpet. The laughter of children playing in pure white snow. Baby chicks in the spring with those little yellow puffs of feathers. A glorious sunrise. A brilliant sunset. The sound of a whippoorwill on a warm summer night. These, and so many more, are right before us to help make our journey enjoyable. God wants us to know that what He created is good— and that He is good! No matter where your life's journey is leading right now, He is there—whether it is a sunny day or a dark night. Remember—the darker the night, the brighter the stars appear.

Even though God created such beauty, He is not a weak God. He is a powerful God who is in control! In the key verse for today, the psalmist is saying just that. God can be trusted to do what needs to be done. He is amazing!

Will you join me today—before we go out the door or start our chores? Let's take time to be still, drink from the Fountain, and let His sweet words remind us of who He is. Maybe today can be the day we stop struggling in our own strength and rest in the reality of His total trustworthiness.

And don't forget to stop and smell the roses along the way!

The Treasure Hunt

"I say this because I know what I am planning for you," says the Lord. "I have good plans for you, not plans to hurt you. I will give you hope and a good future. Then you will call my name. You will come to Me and pray to Me, and I will listen to you. You will search for Me. And when you search for Me with all your heart, you will find Me! I will let you find Me," says the Lord."
Jeremiah 29:11-14a (NCV)

Easter is a wonderful day of celebration. Everyone gets all dressed up in their Sunday best, and the sermon brings such excitement to your heart that you almost understand how Peter and John felt when they saw the empty grave clothes, or the overwhelming joy that Mary felt when the risen Jesus called her by name! And the wonderful music—whether it is a church choir singing an Easter cantata or you singing "Up from the Grave He Arose" with your family in a little country church; it is a time of celebration!

But if you have children in your home, there's one more thing that happens on Easter—the Easter egg hunt! I remember the second Easter after we moved out to the country. My daughters, Rebecca and Emma, were six and two. Before the girls woke up, I was out with two baskets of eggs. Some were thrown out in plain view to make them easy to find. Others were strategically placed in clumps of grass to make it more fun for my oldest daughter. My husband, Dan, came out and said he was hiding the rest, I just needed to give him a few minutes and then send the girls out. So, minutes later here they came—jammie-clad, rubbing their sleepy eyes, empty basket in hand. Dan and I had such fun watching the excitement as their baskets filled with bright-colored eggs filled with tiny treasures. When they thought they had found them all, we counted them. Oops! There were four missing! "I wonder where they could be?", Dan asked. Then, he picked one little girl up, and carried her around the house on his shoulders. "There's one, Daddy! There's another one, Daddy!" Then, he did the same with our other daughter.

What precious memories, and what a beautiful picture of our Heavenly Father's love for us. Just as Dan lifted his precious daughters so they could see more clearly, God lifts us so we can see more clearly. He knows that life isn't always easy. He knows that there are hard times, dark times, and times we think we can't climb one more step up that mountain—yet He is always there! When we take the time and effort, we can find Him there. Whether it's in the sunshine of a beautiful day or hidden from view in the tall grass—He is still there, waiting to be found. And when you just can't find Him on your own, He will lift you up and carry you on His shoulders. He will let you find Him! Oh, what a Savior!

The Destroyer and the Savior

"The devil, your enemy, goes around like a roaring lion looking for someone to eat." I Peter 5:8 (NCV)

"Your love is wonderful. By your power You save those who trust You from their enemies." Psalm 17:7 (NCV)

Home-grown tomatoes. Nothing tastes quite as good as that first juicy, red tomato, fresh-picked from your own garden. And seeing it there on the vine is like finding a treasure. The wait seems long, and there are obstacles along the way; but the wait is so worth it!

The first week after planting those little tomato plants, I discovered the rabbits had made dinner out of an entire tomato plant. I replanted one. Then, day after day, I watched as those little plants grew bigger, stronger, and healthier.

Tiny yellow blooms appeared, then tiny green tomatoes. Then, one day I noticed some of those beautiful, healthy plants had branches that were totally stripped of their leaves and blossoms, leaving only half a tiny green tomato dangling in the air. Then, I saw "them"—those big green hornworms— still feasting! They wouldn't be satisfied till the plant was destroyed. Of course, I couldn't allow that! So, I did just what you would do. I stood and waited for each one, picking them off and destroying them. Their destruction was finished! Then, to prevent them from coming back, I covered their leaves with that wonderful white vegetable dust. Now we are enjoying those beautiful, juicy red tomatoes. They sure can brighten up a dinner table and bring some "zip" to any party as salsa.

Aren't you glad we have a powerful, loving Savior? He is always watching over us. He has already defeated our enemy, the devil. He covered us, not with white dust, but with His precious blood. He stands guard and picks off our enemies. "If we confess our sins, He is faithful and just to forgive us our sins, and to cleanse us from all unrighteousness." (I John 1:9 KJV). He wants us to stay "plugged in" to Him by communication through prayer and reading His word, so we can "bear much fruit". He is for us. He is ever vigilant. He wants us to show this world His love, joy, peace, patience, kindness, goodness, faithfulness, gentleness, and self-control. Oh, what a Savior!

Today, let's keep spreading His Light and Life to a dark and gloomy world.

Making Taffy

"We also have joy with our troubles, because we know that these troubles produce patience. And patience produces character, and character produces hope. And this hope will never disappoint us, because God has poured out his love through the Holy Spirit, whom God has given to us." Romans 5:3-5 (NCV)

When our oldest daughter, Rebecca, turned six years old, she had her first slumber party. It started with pizza for dinner, then dancing to her daddy's banjo, and finally a movie. The living room floor was filled with sleeping bags, pillows, and giggling little girls! It didn't take long until the giggles subsided, and all were fast asleep. After breakfast the next morning they skated in their boots on our shallow pond which was frozen over and snow-covered. After that, everybody came back to the house to warm up with hot chocolate and lunch. Then they were ready for the next adventure—a taffy pull!

Now, coming from a large family, we always had enough kids to have a lot of fun. (And make big messes!) This was the first time we had enough at our house to facilitate such a venture, so we seized the moment to have some good old-fashioned fun with a sweet ending.

After the girls helped me measure the ingredients in my biggest pan, I stirred it on the stove till it was bubbling and clear. Next, each little girl had to butter their hands. Half of them reached in and grabbed a handful of the warm, gooey stuff. The other half of the girls started pulling on the mixture. They pulled back and forth. They folded it over and pulled some more. They kept saying, "It's too hard to pull anymore!" All I could do was encourage them to keep pulling; it would be worth it in the end. "Keep pulling—You'll see!" And they did. Each one had a little bag of the sweet, sticky taffy to take home with them when their parents came to get them. And each one was so excited to tell their parents how they helped make it.

Aren't you thankful for a Heavenly Father who loves us so much that He lets us get in "sticky messes," knowing that He is going to bring something sweet out of them? He never leaves us alone in it. He's always there, encouraging us on. "Keep pulling! You can do it! Don't forget Who lives inside you! It will be worth it all!" He said he'd bring "beauty out of ashes" and give "the oil of joy for mourning."

So, keep pulling! And I'll keep pulling, too. When we keep pulling together, our precious Heavenly Father is making something wonderfully sweet for everyone to enjoy!

Friends

"This is My command: Love each other as I have loved you. The greatest love a person can show is to die for his friends. You are My friends if you do what I command you. I no longer call you servants, because a servant does not know what his master is doing. But I call you friends, because I have made known to you everything I heard from My Father. You did not choose me; I chose you. And I gave you this work: to go and produce fruit, fruit that will last. Then the Father will give you anything you ask for in My name. This is My command: Love each other."
John 15:12-17 (NCV)

Friends make life sweet. They laugh with us. They cry with us. The more of life we share with them, the closer we are to them. They just keep loving us—through the good times and the bad times. Proverbs 17:17 says, "A friend loveth at all times." (KJV).

God has blessed me with many wonderful friends throughout my lifetime, for which I am forever grateful. As Proverbs 27:17 (KJV) says, "Iron sharpeneth iron; so a man sharpeneth the countenance of his friend." I have learned much from my friends. My most precious friend in the whole world is my husband of forty-four years. Believe me, sparks have flown many times as that iron in us has been sharpened! But when the sparks settled, there's no one else I'd rather be with than Dan. We've weathered many storms together. (One literally, as we sat in our little storm cellar together, and heard the tornado go past us!) Yet we've seen lots of sunshine and laughter as we watched our two precious little girls grow up into two beautiful young women inside and out, and now we enjoy six precious grandchildren. Yes, I'm thankful for our friendship here on Earth; but I'm even more thankful that our friendship will not end when we leave this Earth but will continue forever because of our friendship with Jesus.

To think that Jesus chose you and me to be His friends is a wonderful, yet humbling, thought. Jesus—King of Kings, the Creator of the universe, The Beginning and The End—chose us, loves us, and died for us! And He wants us to be with Him forever! What a friend we have in Jesus.

God created us in His image. Therefore, He created us to have friends. He knew we needed each other here on Earth. And He wants us all to be together in Heaven. Let's all go out today and obey His command to love each other.

Heroes

"Very few people will die to save the life of someone else. Although perhaps for a good person someone might possibly die. But God shows His great love for us in this way: Christ died for us while we were still sinners." Romans 5:7-8 (NCV)

We've all had heroes. Little boys called the men on their baseball cards heroes. Little girls called the handsome prince in "Cinderella" their hero. We all know John Wayne was the hero of countless old westerns. George Washington and Abraham Lincoln are the heroes of our country.

My little grandson, Carson, has his own hero—his daddy. How do I know? In 2016, a week prior to Veterans Day, my husband and I took our grandchildren Carson, Rayne, and Khol to the park. Our route took us through downtown Troy, Illinois, where the streets were lined with hundreds of American flags. But what came next was the highlight of the day. Carson (not quite four) explained that those flags were there "for his daddy." His mommy had explained to him earlier they were there to honor all veterans, like his daddy. All Carson heard was they were there for his hero—his daddy. And I think he's right—all those who have given themselves, some even their very lives, for our freedom—should be honored as heroes. Aren't you thankful to live in a country where we can freely worship our wonderful Lord?

Hebrews 11 is full of "heroes of the faith." Abel, Enoch, Noah, Abraham, Isaac, Jacob, Joseph, Moses' parents, Moses, those that crossed the Red Sea, those led by Joshua who marched around Jericho for seven days before the walls fell, Rahab, Gideon, Barak, Samson, Jephthah, David, Samuel, and the prophets. Yes, they are all considered "heroes of the faith."

Now, let's look at our number one Hero. He's bigger than Babe Ruth, Cinderella's prince, John Wayne, George Washington, Abraham Lincoln, Carson's daddy and all our veterans. He's bigger than all those mentioned in Hebrews chapter 11. In fact, He is the Maker of all these heroes. Yet He came to this earth so He could be the Lamb of God. The only One who could give us true, everlasting freedom. The only One who could die for our sins. The sins of every human being. Oh, what a Savior! Oh, what a Hero! My Hero!

Is He your hero?

Another Place, Another Time

> *"God began by making one person, and from him came all the different people who live everywhere in the world. God decided exactly when and where they must live."* Acts 17:26 (NCV)

Pleasant Ridge; a lovely name for a lovely place. It's the place where I grew up. A place where children could walk the rock roads to a little country church on Sunday without fear of being harmed. A place where families gathered around the kitchen table three times a day to share laughter and life, after grace was said over a hot meal consisting mostly of food harvested from the land. A place where families and neighbors gathered yearly to make apple butter and butcher hogs. A place where the social event of the year was the church hayride.

Oh, to be able to go back to that simpler life, to a simpler time! But God didn't make us to stay in one place or time. I thank Him for every precious memory of my childhood, and how each has helped me become who I am today. But aren't you glad God has even more wonderful things in store for us, His children? He has a plan. Every day that passes and every place He moves us is to give us more opportunities to show who Jesus is to a world that needs to "be still and know that He is God." (Psalm 46:10). Setting type in the little print shop at Camp WeWoSeJe was a long, slow process just to get a one-page camp newsletter out.

But today's technology can literally put the entire Bible in the palm of millions of people's hands. The good news that Jesus died for everyone is reaching more people than we could have ever dreamed of! God has given us children and grandchildren to show His love and grace to. And, in turn, they can show His love and grace to many more than we could ever reach by ourselves.

Our dear friends, Norman, and Doris are perfect examples of missionaries. They were always there when their church had an outreach, with all their children in tow. Their children grew up and followed their parents' example. Now, the next generation is doing the same—-all over the country!

Then, there is my dear friend, Mary. When she fell in the yard and ended up with a broken bone, she was excited to be able to share about Jesus with the EMT on the ambulance ride to the hospital. After the hospital stay, she was excited about going to rehab to make new friends with the "lonely ones" there.

I wonder what opportunities God has in store for us today. You know He's up to something good. Let's go out today and live this life He's given us to its fullest and use it up for Him!

Peace and Quiet

"I don't do great things, and I can't do miracles, but I am calm and quiet like a baby with its mother. I am at peace, like a baby with its mother." Psalm 131:1-2 (NCV)

Even grandmothers have bad days. At this season in life, we tend to think life should be a slow nature walk and not a treacherous mountain pass. Your heart is broken. No, beyond broken. It is crushed. And every time you try to continue, life's path seems to be sharp-edged rocks that cut deep into your very soul. The tears start rolling in anticipation of the inevitable pain that comes from trying to move forward. Then, the dreaded voice of the enemy says, "You'll never make it. No good can ever come from your life." Oh, but then I hear the kind, gentle voice of my Heavenly Father say, "Close your eyes and remember. Remember, you are My child." Then, He uses a precious picture in my mind to calm me. I see the picture of my baby holding her baby, and I can say with David: "I don't do great things, and I can't do miracles, but I am calm and quiet like a baby with its mother. I am at peace, like a baby with its mother." (Psalm 131:1-2). Then I open my eyes and I clearly see the next step on the path before me. But, even greater, I see my Jesus taking my hand to lead me on.

My friend, have you been there? Are you there today? Take time today to read His Word. Throughout the entire

Bible, He reminds us over and over how He was with his children. He told them over and over how they could trust Him to go before them, leading the way forward. Don't let the enemy trick you into thinking our God isn't there for you. Over and over, He says: "I will never, never leave you. I will never forsake you." Did you hear that? Never! That means Never!

Now, tell the devil to go back to where he came from.

And never forget—Jesus had a Gethsemane and Calvary. But then, He had an empty tomb. Now He has a seat at the Father's right hand. And what is He doing? Always interceding for us. Did you hear that? Always! That means always! So, lift your head up and follow wherever He leads. It's sure to be a wonderful adventure.

Mending

"God has chosen you and made you his holy people. He loves you. So always do these things; show mercy to others, be kind, humble, gentle, and patient. Get along with each other and forgive each other. If someone does wrong to you, forgive that person because the Lord forgave you. Do all these things; but most important, love each other. Love is what holds you all together in perfect unity. Let the peace that Christ gives control your thinking, because you were all called together in one body to have peace. Always be thankful." Colossians 3:12-15 (NCV)

My husband's flannel shirt was frayed on the shoulder seam; too many times churning in the washing machine, too many times enduring the heat of the dryer. It was too worn out to repair. It would have to be completely taken apart from the lining, making it more vulnerable to fraying. Mending by hand was the only viable option. The old yellow thread box held just what was needed to make the repair: matching navy-blue thread, a needle, and little scissors to clip the thread. The sewing took a little extra time out of my day, but it was well worth it, knowing my husband would be warmed by that old flannel shirt for many more days as he worked out in the cold.

Have you got some mending to do? Have you let the churning inside you or a heated argument fray at the fabric of a relationship? Maybe it's a dear friend or a family member. Maybe you've deemed it unrepairable, or just not worth the effort. Take a second look. Ask God what He sees. He's in the repair business. Isn't that what Calvary is all about? Forgiveness.

Oh, we might be inconvenienced, it might not be easy, or our pride might get hurt. But the joy that comes through sharing life experiences together far surpasses the temporary difficulty. The warmth of a friendship helps when the cold winds of adversity start to blow.

So, after we've prayed, read God's Word, and pray again for His direction—what do we need to do? Get out a pen and paper? Pick up the phone? Get in the car? Whatever we do, let's not let it fall apart from neglect. We need each other.

What's in Your Hands?

"But people are tempted when their own evil desire leads them away and traps them. This desire leads to sin, and then the sin grows and brings death." James 1:14-15 (NCV)

It was a perfect day to play in the cul-de-sac. The heavy rains had ended, the sun was shining, and the temperature was 60 degrees and climbing. What a wonderful break at the end of February! Rayne and Carson both had pants and long sleeves on. Their bike helmets would suffice for protection against the light wind. Khol and Izzy wore light jackets—hoods up and zipped. Rayne rode her bike and drew pretty pictures with sidewalk chalk. Carson rode his bike, played soccer with Khol, and made up a new game. Khol played soccer with Carson then rode his tractor. Izzy was content to ride leisurely around in circles in her little red car (powered by grandma), laughing with the other kids, and enjoying the sun on her tiny face. Everyone was enjoying the day of play. After an hour or so, I noticed that Izzy started getting bored and proceeded to unzip her jacket and pull her hood down. I instructed her to put her hood up and zip her jacket. Off we went for another loop. She unzipped the jacket and pulled the hood down again. A battle of wills ensued, and I had to instruct her on every loop. Good thing it was time for lunch and a nap! Everyone was ready to go in, but even if we weren't, I would have taken Izzy in to spare her an earache from the cold temperature.

Remember your Sunday School teacher or your mama saying, "Idle hands are the devil's workshop?" Sweet Izzy was engaging in behavior that, gone unchecked, could ultimately end in a lot of pain from an inevitable earache.

Now, look at your hands. What are they involved in? Are they just idle? Our wonderful Lord has a good plan for all of us. Read Ephesians 2:10. He has something good for us to be doing. He "deployed" us when He gave the Great Commission. He tells us to encourage one another, show His love and kindness, meet others' needs, do our part in the body of Christ, and work to provide for our families. Need He say more? Working for the King of Kings is a wonderful privilege! What work has He put in your hands today?

Can You Hear It?

"The Lord your God is with you; the Mighty One will save you. He will rejoice over you. You will rest in His love; He will sing and be joyful about you." Zephaniah 3:17 (NCV.)

Remember those old, sweet love songs written to Jeannie, Tammy, Barbara, Corinna, Sherry, Bonnie, Charlotte, Darlene, Georgia, Hannah (oops! Maybe hard-hearted is not such a term of endearment!), Irene, Rose, Elizabeth...the list goes on and on, but I think you get the picture. My husband, Dan, even wrote a sweet little song about me when we were dating. My heart melted when he brought his guitar over and sang it to me. I knew he had been thinking about me and loved me, and that I was precious to him.

Now, remember all those little songs we sang over our children and grandchildren? Why did we do it? Because we love them. We think about them. We want them to know the joy they bring to us. And we want them to feel safe and secure in our love for them.

Isn't this verse from Zephaniah a beautiful picture of God's love for His children? When we accept His plan of salvation He adopts us as His children—His very own children! Over and over in His Word, He tells us how He delights in us. Even as much as our husbands love us, and we love our children and grandchildren, none can compare with His love for us! His love is greater, stronger, and more powerful than we could ever imagine! He created us. Knowing that real love is a choice, He gave us a free will. Knowing we would be tempted and sin, He already had a plan to redeem us—the death of His precious, only-begotten Son on a cruel cross. Oh, what love He showed there! How deep His love is for us. What a concert He must have given as Jesus rose from the dead, and as Jesus came back to Heaven to sit at His Father's right hand!

Scripture says that the angels rejoice when a sinner comes to the Father. How much more precious it is to know that our Father is rejoicing over us, His adopted children, with singing! Take time today to open His word and read. Can you hear Him rejoicing?

Pictures

"So God created human beings in his image. In the image of God he created them. He created them male and female." Genesis 1:27 (NCV)

"If anyone belongs to Christ, there is a new creation. The old things have gone; everything is made new!" II Corinthians 5:17 (NCV)

We love pictures! We have pictures on every wall of our house. We have several pictures from friends, reminding Dan and I that they are praying for us. We have one picture reminding us of a wonderful vacation. We have a farm scene, complete with cotton ball clouds created by our youngest daughter when she was in first grade. We have a beautiful painting done by our oldest daughter when she was in college titled "The Singer's Shoes"—a picture of her daddy's old cowboy boots. The other pictures that cover our walls, shelves, dressers, end tables, and coffee tables are pictures of our family. There are school pictures, graduation pictures, and wedding pictures. Family pictures—from black and white grandma and grandpa pictures to colored mom and dad pictures, to daughter pictures, to grandchildren pictures. I think you get the picture—pun intended!

Now, I'll let you in on a little secret. When I dust the pictures on the piano, I can't help myself. I kiss all six of my precious grandchildren's faces, then hold them close to my heart, and pray that Jesus holds each one close to Him, protects them, and guides them on their life's journey. And as I do, my heart is comforted, and I thank God for the blessing of having them in my life.

It came as no surprise to me when little one-and-a-half-year-old Izzy was drawn like a magnet to the coffee table. At eye-level was a picture of her and her family. Once discovered, she smiled from ear to ear, pointed at each one, and jabbered on and on, as only a toddler can. It sure made nap time easier after her discovery!

I wonder who needs to see a picture of Jesus today? Not an artist's idea of what He looked like when He walked this earth, but His image coming from one of His own—you and me. Do you think someone needs to remember they have an older brother who loves them enough to die for them? And that He is always with them, in their heart?

Don't forget, we need to keep our picture of Jesus at eye-level—Just like He did.

Smile, He's watching you!

Father's Love

"The Lord himself will give you a sign: The virgin will be pregnant. She will have a son, and she will name him Immanuel." Isaiah 7:14 (NCV)

As I write this, tomorrow is Fathers' Day. I am thinking about my daddy. Daddy was a night watchman at the mill in town. When he came home each morning, he spent time reading his Bible at the table and praying on his knees in the kitchen. Then, he would wake the kids up. We'd come downstairs to a hot breakfast and a pot of hot tea on the stove. After getting us out the door to catch the school bus, he'd milk the cow, feed the chickens, gather the eggs, and slop the hogs. He did all this before getting some sleep after a long night of work. Yet, in the evenings, he always had time to play a game of dominoes, checkers, Chinese checkers, or dot-to-dot with his kids. (Now that I'm older, I realize that he didn't just **have** time, he **made** time!)

Of all the games we played and all the stories he told, one moment stands out above the rest. It was the spring of 1957. After my older siblings had all left for school and Daddy had done his chores, he took me on the highly anticipated "mushroom hunt." You know what I'm talking about, searching for those mouth-watering morels God grows in the woods for the deer and the humans. What an adventure Daddy shared with me! And what a treat to enjoy fried mushrooms and eggs at breakfast the next morning.

Even if we only had one mushroom to split between us, the sheer delight of a walk through the woods with my daddy was well worth it!

Now, fast-forward to 1986. Dan and I lived in the country. Although Daddy didn't get out much, he couldn't resist a mushroom hunt on our land. The walk through the woods and the time shared with my daddy will always be precious to me.

My daddy has since gone on to be with The Lord, but I treasure all the memories of the precious time spent with him. I trust that you, too, have many precious memories of life shared with your daddy. And, if your daddy is still living, I trust that you will make many more precious memories together.

Now, let's think about our Heavenly Father, who wanted to be with us so much that He said Mary would give birth to Immanuel—which means "God with us." Then, when Jesus ascended to Heaven, He said He would send the Holy Spirit to not only live with us, but in us. He said He'd never leave us or forsake us. And, when He comes again, we will all rise to meet Him in the air. He will take us to Heaven. We will be with Him forever. What a God! What a Father! What a Dad!

If you didn't know a daddy like mine, you can still know the love of the Father—a perfect love. He's waiting with arms open wide, ready to share in all your days here and for all eternity!

Apples and Understanding

"...Peace be with you." John 20:19 (NCV)

"...Come and eat." John 21:12 (NCV)

"...Follow Me!" John 21:19 (NCV)

My husband and I were blessed to share company with 20-month-old Izzy and her big brother, Carson, for the weekend. After making precious memories on Friday evening and Saturday, we left for church Sunday morning. It was a quiet ride until Izzy started singing. Her sweet little voice made a song out of one word. Over and over, she sang: "Apple, apple, apple." Now, don't get me wrong, Izzy has a lot to say, but most of it is not in the same language you and I are familiar with. Toddlerish. Yet Izzy has mastered several words that are important to her: Mom, Dad, Khol, Rayne, Carson, baby, bath, water, and apple. Yes, Izzy loves her family, she loves to play in the water, and she loves apples! So, it came as no surprise that she would sing a sweet little song about apples. Sounds like apples not only make her tummy happy, but her heart happy, too!

Now, let's go back two thousand years. Jesus' disciples have come together and locked themselves in a room. They were afraid of what the Jews would do to them. Did Jesus leave them alone in their fear? No! He came to them.

He spoke four simple words: "Peace be with you." They understood. He would never leave them. He even came back a week later with those same precious four words: "Peace be with you." Even doubting Thomas understood that Jesus would never leave him.

When Peter and John first met Jesus, they were fishing. That was their livelihood before meeting Jesus (you could say it paid the bills). So, it's no surprise that Peter got a fishing trip together. After exhausting themselves from fishing all night and catching absolutely nothing, they heard a man on the shore call to them: "Friends, did you catch any fish?" (John 21:4) The man then instructed them to throw the net on the other side of the boat. They did, and voila! There was enough to pay the bills, with plenty to share! Then, Jesus simply tells them to come eat with Him. They all knew it was Jesus, and they all knew they could trust Him to meet their needs.

The last scene in John chapter 21 shows Jesus talking to Peter. Jesus not only extends His grace and forgiveness for all three times Peter denied Him, but offers Peter (and all of us) guidance and purpose with two simple words: "Follow Me."

Dear friend, where are you today? Are you fearful? Have circumstances caused you to doubt the Truth? Have you "blown it"? Has "your way" gotten you nowhere? Follow Jesus' lead. Spend time with Him. He doesn't make it hard. Listen. Learn. Understand.

"Peace be with you."

The Gift of Color

"How precious also are thy thoughts unto me, O God! How great is the sum of them! If I should count them, they are more in number than the sand: when I awake, I am still with thee." Psalm 139:17-18 (KJV)

Remember when you were a little kid, and your mom and dad took you to see Santa? I sure do. Back in the 50's, Santa had three standard gifts—a candy cane, a small coloring book, and a small magic box filled with three crayons. We could hardly wait to get back to the car so we could start eating our candy canes and create beautiful Christmas masterpieces. What sweet memories!

But Christmas 2018 gave me even sweeter memories. Miss Mary had given my four youngest grandchildren giant coloring books. Two-year-old Izzy had started her masterpiece—a picture of Mr. Mouse on a Christmas ornament. Six-year-old Rayne asked if she could help, and the two girls colored away. The finished product was beautiful! I've never seen a Christmas ornament with quite so many colors. I believe they used every color from the sixty-four-crayon box!

Are you like me? Does color bring you joy? The Lord must think so because He gave us too many colors to count. Have you seen a sunrise or sunset lately? He must use nearly all the colors on His palette! There are all the different-colored birds: yellow canaries, bluebirds, red cardinals, red-breasted robins; even those little gray, black, and white chickadees with tiny yellow bellies. And what about the flowers? There are yellow daffodils, autumn leaves, orange butterfly plants, blue bachelor buttons, and roses of nearly every hue—from pale pink to bright red.

And what about those beautiful rainbows God puts in the sky after a rain? Even more precious than the beautiful show of color is the reason why God puts it there. Genesis 9:14-16 (NCV) says, "When I bring clouds over the earth and a rainbow appears in them, I will see it and I will remember the agreement that continues forever between me and every living thing on the earth." What love! What grace! What mercy!

This brings us to another color. Have you let God use His most precious color—the crimson red flow from Calvary— to wash away your sins? Only then will you know the inexpressible joy that comes from knowing Him and to truly enjoy all the beauty of His colorful creation.

Are You Still In?

"Paul stayed two full years in his own rented house and welcomed all people who came to visit him. He boldly preached about the kingdom of God and taught about the Lord Jesus Christ, and no one tried to stop him." Acts 28:30-31 (NCV)

Have you ever felt like you were put on the sidelines and not really in the game? Today, that's where I'm at. I'd much rather be walking up and down our road, enjoying the beautiful, snow-covered landscape. Instead, I'm stuck inside due to a glaze of ice and temperatures stuck below 20 degrees. My only exercise today is from the stationary bicycle in my warm home. It is no comparison to the encouraging conversation my walking buddy and I share as we enjoy God's wonderful creation.

Just keep pedaling. Do what you can, where you can.

As I pedaled, I couldn't help but ponder these last two verses in Acts. After just finishing reading this action-packed book covering Paul's adventures, I noticed his zeal for telling the good news was still there, despite the hardship. When Paul saw Jesus, The Light, on the way to Damascus Paul followed. Everywhere Paul went, Paul preached Jesus. Paul preached Jesus to Gentiles, to kings, and to Jews.

And then, at the end of Acts, Paul was in custody and still shared Jesus with everyone around him. God's plan was still working!

So, it is today—God's plan is still working. What we plan may or may not be working, but His plan is always working!

Are you put "on the sidelines" due to the weather, sickness, or circumstances beyond your control? Remember, God is in control. Let's keep doing what we can, where we can. Only time will tell what good God has done in our "off times."

Have a good news day!

He'll Keep You Afloat

"...He says, 'Don't be afraid, because I have saved you. I have called you by name, and you are mine. When you pass through the waters, I will be with you. When you cross rivers, you will not drown. When you walk through fire, you will not be burned, nor will the flames hurt you."
Isaiah 43:1-2 (NCV)

"Where God's love is, there is no fear, because God's perfect love drives out fear..." 1 John 4:18 (NCV)

I was watching from the pool deck as four-and-a-half-year-old twins, Carson and Rayne, were thoroughly enjoying the hot summer day by jumping in the pool, swimming to the steps, clamoring up the steps, laughing, and trying to see who could get to the other side of the deck first. Little two-year-old Khol sat on the pool steps, playing with a water gun. When Rayne got a little too close for comfort, she was met with a scowl and Khol said, "No, Rayne!" Although all three were clad with floaties, Khol just wasn't sure his would keep his head above water. Fear was holding him back.

Everything changed when their mommy got in the pool. She smiled at Khol, reached out her arms, and said "Come here, Kholie Bear!" That's all it took! He leaped off the steps. When his face came right up out of the water, I believe his smile could have brightened up the whole neighborhood. Cheers and "high fives" came from his cheering section. His big brother said, "Come on, buddy, jump with me and Rayne!" Khol took Carson's outstretched hand, and off they went—running, jumping, and laughing together.

What a beautiful picture of what Jesus can do in our lives when we know He's close. We can trust Him to keep us afloat, no matter how difficult the trials and troubles get. He is always nearby. He goes before us, stands behind us, holds our right hand, and has taken up permanent residence in our hearts when we trust Him to be our Lord and Savior! His Word assures us of His presence in our lives. We are His children and the "apple of His eye". And what joy He brings when we fully trust Him.

Are you sitting on the steps today? When He says, "Come here, I've got something better for you," trust Him.

He wouldn't ask you to do it if He wasn't going to give you the ability to do it. Take the plunge! You've got your own world to brighten up with His love.

Let's go swimming!

Mulberry Trees—What Do They Say to You?

> *"And let it be, when thou hearest the sound of a going in the tops of the mulberry trees, that then thou shalt bestir thyself: for then shall the Lord go out before thee, to smite the host of the Philistines. And David did so, as the Lord had commanded him: and smote the Philistines from Geba until thou come to Gazer."* 2 Samuel 5:24-25 (KJV)

A few days ago, God reminded me of a song that I had not heard since I was a teenager. The chorus says, "The move is on, I know the move is on; for I can hear the rustling in the mulberry trees, and I know, I know, the move is on." This song set off a sweet memory from my childhood.

As a child, I grew up on a 40-acre farm where my daddy grew all sorts of vegetables, strawberries, and gooseberries. Besides what Daddy had planted, the land was blessed with wild blackberries and sweet mulberries. We had an old tin cup which we had to use for harvesting and consuming the purple delights. One of us would take the old cup to the mulberry tree, pick berries, put sugar and cream on them, and then quickly devour the tasty treat before handing the cup to the next child. Each child did the same until we all had purple hands and mouths that were happy, happy, happy. What fun it was to share life with my brothers and sisters. How good it was to know that our Heavenly Father had blessed us with such a wonderful treat!

Now, listen to the story of David. David had spent many years tending to his father's sheep. All the while, he was talking and listening to God. They had built a relationship of trust. He asked for God's direction and listened when God gave it. David knew he could count on God to communicate with him.

Eventually, David became the King of Israel. He still asked God for direction because he knew that God would defeat the enemy. So, David asked if he should go into battle with the enemy. Right away David heard God's answer: "Don't attack the enemy from the front. Instead, go around and attack them in front of the mulberry trees. When you hear marching in the tops of the trees, act quickly. I, the Lord, will have gone ahead of you to defeat the Philistine army." So, David did what the Lord commanded. He defeated the Philistines and chased them all the way from Gibeon to Gazer." (2 Samuel 5:24-25) Wow! God communicated the sound of victory, the sound of faithfulness, to take care of His children once again.

So, what is God saying to you today? He's already made the way for you. You can trust Him. Just step out in faith.

Mm! Think I'll go find me an old tin cup.

Gift Baskets

"This is the day that the Lord has made. Let us rejoice and be glad today!" Psalm 118:24 (NCV)

At Christmas in 2019 we made several gift baskets to give to family and friends. Each one was custom made based on what we knew everyone enjoyed. My husband and I were thrilled to add our own home-canned zucchini relish, salsa, peppers, apple butter, and jelly. Then, we added home-made deer sausage, accompanied by cheese and crackers, a bag of tortilla chips, soft peppermints, and chocolate kisses. We wrapped everything in pretty Christmas paper. It brought joy to our hearts to be able to share something special that we had made.

All of this made me think about how God must feel when I open my "present" of each new day. Do I bring joy to His heart? Do I put a smile on His face? Do I thank Him for those special things He has put into this day? Or is it something special to build character in me? And do I thank Him for those special little surprises? Maybe it's not candy, but a little blue bird or red cardinal, golden yellow leaves, a juicy red tomato, the smile of a grandma, the laughter of a child, a kiss from my husband, a golden sunrise, a gorgeous sunset, ice on the bare winter tree branches glimmering in the sun, pure white snow, or words of encouragement from a friend. I could fill a book with precious signs of "I love you" from the Lord, but I'll let you make your own list.

Oh, how He loves us to continue to bless us with present after present. Our Father delights in giving us what we need and provides us joy during the days.

May we always unwrap everything He has for us. May we never be so preoccupied with the next present that we miss the special little things He has for us today.

Think about that the next time you put a soft peppermint in your mouth!

Play Dough

"But Lord, you are our father. We are like clay, and you are the potter; your hands made us all."
Isaiah 64:8 (NCV)

Preschooler Khol and toddler Izzy didn't mind the rainy afternoon. They had play dough! They created everything from an octopus to a giraffe. I found such joy in watching their happy faces as they formed that play dough into just the right shape.

The play dough creation kit included the octopus mold, which, when filled with play dough and pressed down, caused legs to magically appear. The giraffe was formed using a cookie cutter, making every one of them look the same. But both little ones thought it was much more fun to make them by hand. Before they were done playing, Khol decided he would put all the colors together. The not-so-pretty gray/brown color was not quite what he expected.

Think about the pressure it took to form the octopus' legs. Have you ever wondered why you had to go through such hard trials, only to be amazed by the strength our Father gave you to move forward?

Think about the cookie cutter giraffes. Aren't you thankful that God didn't create everyone the same? All the way to thumbprints—no two are the same! Ephesians 4:11 tells us God has given us all different gifts as different parts of the body of Christ. And, as we all do our own work, the whole body grows and is strengthened by love. Just as my grandchildren love creating their own version of a giraffe, so our Creator has made us all just the way He wants, to be used in the right place at just the right time.

To be beautiful on the inside, we must grow into who God created us to be. We also need to keep the brightness of Jesus shining from our hearts. We must not let temptations in, no matter how colorful they may seem at the time. In the end, our hearts seem to be a dingy, gray/brown. Then we can cry out to the Lord as David did in Psalm 51:10-12, "Create in me a pure heart, God, and make my spirit right again. Give me back the joy of your salvation." Khol couldn't make the colors all come out and leave only bright yellow, but Jesus can do that to our hearts. Today, won't you soften to His touch and let Him mold you into that beautiful, useful creation that will shine and bring Him glory?

Laughter

"A happy heart is like good medicine, but a broken spirit drains your strength." Proverbs 17: 22 (NCV)

We were all sitting around the table with play dough in the middle. Carson and Khol were both making "play dough" hair for their little minions. Rayne was making princess dresses. Grandma, with Izzy in her arms, was making accessories for the dresses. Everyone was talking and laughing, while little Izzy just watched with a smile on her face. Then it happened! Three-month-old Izzy broke out in what her mommy calls a belly laugh. You know, the kind that comes from down in your belly and spreads infectiously to everyone else in the room. What sheer delight!

Obviously, we were programmed for laughter—to enjoy life! Have you forgotten how to laugh? Have you forgotten how laughter puts a spring in your step for the rest of the day? Ecclesiastes 8:15 says to "Enjoy life, because these joys will help you do the hard work God gives you to do here on Earth." God didn't promise an easy path, but He did promise joy for the journey! Remember that God thought joy was so important, that it was the second fruit of the Spirit.

Balance life out. Don't just "weep with those that weep," but also "be happy with those who are happy,"(Romans 12:15) and laugh with those who laugh!

So, go ahead-smile with Him today-you know He's smiling at you!

Encouragers

"They helped everyone his neighbor; and every one said to his brother, Be of good courage."
Isaiah 41:6 (KJV)

"God has made us what we are. In Christ Jesus, God made us to do good works, which God planned in advance for us to live our lives doing." Ephesians 2: 10 (NCV)

We all need encouragement. Sometimes we need it just to make it through the day, sometimes we need it to do a monumental task. God knows our needs. Just as He promised in His Word, He supplies "encouragers" just when we need them.

I have been blessed abundantly by marrying such an encourager. Throughout the past forty-four years of our lives together, I have watched God work through this precious man, ministering encouragement to young and old alike. He was my coach through natural childbirth classes and the birth of both our daughters. He took walks with me to prepare for their births. When both girls were old enough to have an interest in music, he made sure they had piano lessons—and that they didn't quit even when they tried. He encouraged our girls while they learned to horseback ride, play softball and volleyball, create artwork, perform well in school, and hunt deer. Most of all, he encouraged them to have a relationship with Jesus by taking them to church. He even took our family on a mission trip.

His encouragement did not stop with our girls but has continued with our grandchildren and many others. God has used him to encourage many children to be their best through his involvement in Sunday school, 4H, Royal Ambassadors, guitar lessons, and even preschool soccer. They knew they could do it if "Mr. Dan" was there!

My Dan has been my greatest encourager in life. He encouraged me when I started a new job, a new hobby, and when I decided to write this devotional.

I hope you have a great encourager like Dan in your life. But, even more, I hope you have *The Great Encourager* in your life. I can't imagine life without Dan, but I'm so thankful we both have Jesus in our hearts to encourage our hearts with His Word. John 14:26 says that the Comforter (the Holy Spirit) will bring the words He has said for us to our remembrance. The Bible is chock-full of encouragement. I encourage you to read it today. It will come back to you when you need it.

Is there someone in your life that needs some encouragement? Maybe, just maybe, God could use you today!

Children and Eagles

> *"Even children become tired ·and need to rest, and young people trip and fall. But the people who trust The Lord will become strong again. They will rise up as an eagle in the sky, they will run and not need rest; they will walk and not become tired." Isaiah 40: 30-31 (NCV)*

Nap time was never easy for my oldest daughter, Rebecca. She always said, "I don't need a nap, I'm not sleepy!" The funny thing was, when she got quiet and closed her eyes, she was soon fast asleep. Emma, our youngest, always seemed to welcome naptime. Both girls had the same outcome from nap time, they were recharged for a wonderful rest of the day.

Are you like me and become spiritually tired? Do you get worn out from trouble in the world or your personal life? Psalm 37:7 in the King James Version says, "Rest in the Lord, and wait patiently for Him." Resting, waiting, and trusting form a beautiful trio in the song of our everyday lives. Jesus invites us to find rest in Him regardless of the circumstances that surround us. I look forward to my morning "rest" with Him. He is precious to me, and He reminds me that I am precious to Him. He also reminds me how much He loves all of us, His creation. He doesn't want any of us to miss out on eternal life or an abundant life on Earth!

Don't cheat yourself of your "time of rest" in His presence. Time with the Lord makes a great difference in your life and may make "all" the difference in someone else's life. Please don't miss out on the rest of your great adventure.

And remember, when the load you're carrying is left at His feet, you are light enough to soar like an eagle, run to the finish line, and follow Him wherever He leads!

Grandma Maida's Scrapbook

First Family Photo

Daddy, me, and sis Marlene

Mama and me

Mama's Dumplings

Dumplings
1 egg to 1 cup broth
flour enough
to roll
salt, pepper
put enough flour
in hot broth to
make paste add
egg beat good add
flour enough to roll.
approx. 2 cups flour
to 1 cup broth more
or less.

Dan and me then

The young Dan Carson family

Dan and me now

Our daughters

Rebecca 7 years

Emma 3 years

Nap time with Papa

Wyatt

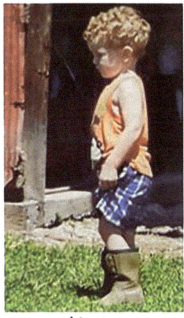

Mason

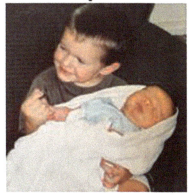

Wyatt & Mason

Carson, Rayne, Baby Khol

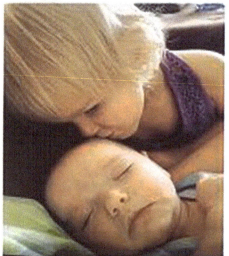

Carson

Khol

Grandma
&
Her Girls

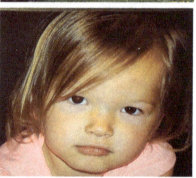

Gods answer for peace.

Precious little hands

Refrigerator art

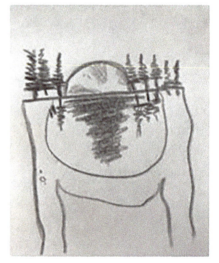

Apples by Noel

God is my shield   Reminder of His love

A Daddy's Love

> *"The Spirit we received does not make us slaves again to fear; it makes us children of God. With that Spirit we cry out, "Father" (literally, "Abba, Father"). And the Spirit himself joins with our spirits to say we are God's children."*
> Romans 8: 15-16 (NCV)

Our dear friends, Ronnie and Cindy, were our first visitors after I left the hospital. After giving me a few days to recover from surgery, Cindy was anxious to bring a delicious, hot meal (with wonderful leftovers, I might add!). And the visit meant so much to my family.

Dan had been taking good care of me. He had taken care of the laundry, the dishes, and kept the house clean. I don't know what I'd do without him. But when they came over, Cindy noticed something she thought I needed. My chair provided a clear view out the living room window, and she thought I needed a hummingbird feeder attached to the outside of that window. But God had already brought such an array of birds to my window, I didn't even need it! Every day of my recovery He sent birds of every size and color just for me to enjoy. They are precious reminders of His thoughts toward me. Daily blessings from my Heavenly Daddy.

Remember those tiny treats your daddy gave you when you were little? You know the feeling of sheer delight you get as a mommy or daddy (or grandma or grandpa) when you give tiny treats to your children (or grandchildren)? Please know that our Heavenly Daddy delights in giving us tiny treats. Oh, how He delights in us—to send His one and only precious Son into our world to bear all our sin and shame on an undeserved cross! Have you accepted His lavish love? Have you let Him adopt you as His own child? Don't wait! He's waiting with arms open wide to receive you into His family. The King of all Kings wants us to be His children!

Once you are His, keep your eyes and ears open.

You never know what "tiny treats" He will send your way.

What's Goin' On?!

"What shall we then say to these things? If God be for us, who can be against us?" Romans 8: 31 (KJV)

"Yes, I am sure that neither death, nor life, not angels, nor ruling spirits, nothing now, nothing in the future, no powers, nothing above us, nothing below us, nor anything else in the whole world will ever be able to separate us from the love of God that is in Christ Jesus our Lord." Romans 8: 38-39 (NCV)

One Friday evening, when my grandson Wyatt was two years old, my husband and I took Wyatt on a shopping trip. It was nothing out of the ordinary. We were riding along, taking in the scenery, and enjoying one another's company. Suddenly, PaPa Dan remembered something, quickly pulled off the street into a parking lot and stopped abruptly. Before I could say anything, Wyatt blurted out "What doin' on?" At that sweet age, his "g's" were always "d's." Wyatt knew his PaPa Dan loved him and wouldn't do anything to cause him harm, but he wanted no part of something he didn't think was quite necessary! PaPa Dan responded "Sorry, buddy, I forgot something, and the brakes work a little too good, it's okay," and trust came back to Wyatt's face.

Have you ever been going down life's road, just enjoying the journey, and felt like you were thrown into something? Life happens, and fear rises. It is easy to question God, but how much sooner we could get back to enjoying the journey if we just stopped and listened to His Word.

Nothing can separate us from His love. No sudden stops. No bumps in the road. Nothing. Let that sweet smile return to your face and reassurance come back into your heart. Let's enjoy the journey together with Him.

"You Never Know!"

"So don't worry about tomorrow, because tomorrow will have its own worries. Each day has enough trouble of its own." Matthew 6: 34 (NCV)

" ...and I will be with you always, even until the end of this age." Matthew 28: 20 (NCV)

Grandchildren are such a blessing! They say some of the sweetest things and they can speak truth without realizing how profound their words are. When little Mason was four years old, he had picked up a phrase that he would say frequently. One afternoon he was in a conversation with PaPa Dan. It sounded as if Mason only responded to questions with "You never know, PaPa, you never know!" It sounded so cute, and we all found laughter in the phrase, but how true it is! We never know what tomorrow will hold.

If we knew what tomorrow would bring, how would we react? Would we freeze in fear? Pull the covers over our head and go back to bed? Often, on the hard days, we miss our time with the Lord and don't have the instructions to make it through. Maybe we even miss the good we can do in someone else's life.

If we could see the future, I am afraid of how we would react. Would we be so overcome with joyful anticipation at our own good fortune, that we would lose sight ·of what God has for us today? Would we be so preoccupied with "me" that we'd forget about those placed in our path to love?

Aren't you glad that our wise, all-knowing Heavenly Father gives us the gift of twenty-four hours every day? No more, no less. And He gives us His Word that He will be with us no matter what. Even though we don't know what each day holds, we can rest and trust that God knows and cares.

The Real Princess Dress

> "The Father hos loved us so much that we are called children of God. And we really are his children." 1 John 3:1 (NCV)

> "God, your thoughts are precious to me. They are so many! If I could count them, they would be more than all the grains of sand. When I wake up, I am still with you." Psalm 139:17-19 (NCV)

It was the night of the church lock-in for young children so their parents could have a free night. The boys could dress up like soldiers and act out Bible stories, and the girls were having a princess tea party. All the girls were to dress up in their favorite princess costume. (Remember Rayne and all her princess dresses? She was excited for this event!) Mom asked Rayne which princess costume she wanted to wear. Rayne's eager reply was, "Belle!" This was Rayne's affectionate nickname for her yellow Easter dress. Her mom tried to convince her to wear a traditional Disney dress, but Rayne would not change her mind.

Rayne loved the dress because of the meaning behind it. When time came for Rayne's Easter shopping trip, her mom couldn't go, so daddy took his "little princess" instead. She didn't care what anyone else would have thought. It was her princess dress, bought by daddy for his "little princess!"

Do you remember who you are? You became a child of The King when you accepted Jesus. Isaiah 61:10 says, " I will greatly rejoice in the Lord, my soul shall be joyful in my God; for He hath clothed me with the garments of salvation, He hath covered me with the robe of righteousness, as a bridegroom decketh himself with ornaments, and as a bride adorneth herself with her jewels." How much more "regal" can you get? He sees us as His children and loves us as His own.

Oh, yes, even though mom had to wash little Rayne's princess dress right after the party, Rayne knew she was still her daddy's little princess.

What Do You See?

"He gives food to cattle and to the little birds that call." Psalm 147:9 (NCV)

"Look at the birds. They don't plant or harvest, they don't have storerooms or barns, but God feeds them. And you are worth much more than birds." Luke 12:24 (NCV)

On the way to church we saw them. They literally covered the roadside between our house and the neighbor's field. Dandelions! Although I think they look like droplets of sunshine, they did not appear the same to Dan. He knew that no matter how "cute" they were, they could easily overtake a yard. Naturally, Dan said, "Guess I'll have to put weedkiller on my list."

Fast forward two days. After my morning devotions, I looked out my living room window to meditate on God's goodness before starting my daily tasks. Then, I saw them! They also looked like droplets of sunshine, only this time they were flying! A half-dozen goldfinches had migrated to the fence across the road. One by one, they flew down off the fence and onto—you guessed it—those same pesky dandelions! God had given them nourishment and brought me great pleasure.

What little "droplets of Sonshine" have you been given lately? Watching a lovely rose unfold? An unexpected note from a friend? A phone call? A visit when loneliness had almost overtaken you? A baby's laughter? A hug from your child or grandchild? A beautifully manicured lawn? That beautiful passage of Scripture that spoke straight to your heart? Oh, how He loves us!

We all need sunshine for our physical health, they say. How much more we need "Sonshine" for our spiritual, mental, and emotional health, as well. I'm sure you thank Him every day for the light His Son shines on you. And I'm sure you have already been given ways to spread His Sonshine to someone else. Isn't He awesome?

By the way, those same finches have hung around. They still sit on the fence across the road. Only this time they are feasting on the neighbor's cover-crop of wheat. Remember—He's always there and He always cares!

What Did You Learn in Sunday School?

"...It is better to obey than to sacrifice..." 1 Samuel 15: 22 (NCV)

Every child blessed to go through Mrs. Clore's Junior Sunday School Class at Pleasant Ridge Union Church knows this Scripture. They can quote it nearly sixty years later. I should know. I was one of those children. We said it every Sunday morning. No matter what our Sunday school lesson was on, it always came down to obedience. Whether it was Saul's lack of obedience, Deborah's victory in battle, or Gideon's victory with an outnumbered army; it all came down to obedience. God had a plan. If people listened and obeyed, their lives and the lives of their people would be blessed.

Mrs. Clore taught us to obey our parents, our teachers, our elders, and all those who had authority over us. But above all that, she taught us to obey God because He knows what's best for all of us. He sees yesterday, today, tomorrow, and every day thereafter.

Mrs. Clore also taught us that we could have fun and enjoy one another's company while we served the Lord. I remember meeting the rest of the Sunday school class at the church on Pleasant Ridge. Mrs. Clore would be there with brooms, dustpans, dust rags, and furniture polish. She always brought a basket of sandwiches, chips, cookies, and some mason jars filled with cold sweet tea. What a treat! We all worked as hard as we could so we could get to the fun—a picnic and fellowship with our friends.

As I am writing this, one of Mrs. Clore's favorite hymns keeps going over in my mind. You probably know it. "Trust and obey for there's no other way to be happy in Jesus, but to trust and obey."

Precious memories from a simpler, slower-paced time. But today's junior Sunday school class still needs those same lessons from the same precious Word of God. And the Lord is still looking for more teachers like Mrs. Clore. Listen close, He might be calling you!

Miss Emilee

"You made my whole being; You formed me in my mother's body. I praise you because you made me in an amazing and wonderful way. What You have done is wonderful. I know this very well. You saw my bones being formed as I took shape in my mother's body. When I was put together there, you saw my body as it was formed. All the days planned for me were written in Your book before I was one day old. God, Your thoughts are precious to me. They are so many!" Psalm 139: 13-17 (NCV)

Miss Emilee is the embodiment of the sweet innocence of a child and the unconditional love of The Father. She will forever be her mommy and daddy's little girl, and God's messenger of love to her world. For thirty-three years Miss Emilee has been fulfilling her calling—to make people feel loved.

Miss Emilee couldn't run with the other kids because of physical limitations. She couldn't play board games because of mental limitations. But her mommy and daddy saw how she loved to put jigsaw puzzles together. Soon, Miss Emilee had her very own puzzle library, bringing hours of enjoyment to her precious life.

Her mommy and daddy soon discovered family vacations weren't much fun for Emilee. Since being unfamiliar with the surroundings brought more fear than fun. They decided to buy a camper, which opened a whole new world for her. With familiar surroundings to come back to after a day's adventure, she could enjoy each day with her family. Her enjoyment only multiplied as friends started camping along with them.

Miss Emilee has been the county's Special Olympics Bowling Champion for several years in a row. She goes to work at the local shop every Monday through Friday. She loves her family and friends, and lives a rich, full life.

Not long ago I was shopping at the local grocery store. As I was getting ready to turn down an aisle, I heard Miss Emilee call out the familiar "Mamie!" She was so excited she could hardly wait to engulf me in one of her famous hugs. All the troubles and sorrows of the day just melted away as Miss Emilee completed her mission. I felt loved. I felt special.

Oh, to see people as God sees them. This old world could sure use more hearts like Miss Emilee's, don't you think?

Rainbows

"When I bring clouds over the earth and a rainbow appears in them, I will remember my agreement between me and you and every living thing." Genesis 9: 14 (NCV)

"For God so loved the world, that He gave His only begotten Son, that whosoever believeth in Him should not perish, but have everlasting life." John 3:16 (KJV)

The rain was coming down as we pulled out of little Wyatt's driveway. I hoped it would stop by the time we got home; about forty-five minutes down the road. Rain could sure put a damper on the outdoor fun of a two-year-old on PaPa and Grandma's farm. But God had a plan. About half-way home, the rain started letting up, the sun came out, and right before us was the biggest, brightest, double rainbow we had ever seen. It was as though we were driving right into it. I was in awe of the majesty of God to create such beauty. But I'll never forget Wyatt's face; his eyes were wide open with a child-like sense of awe and wonder! I'm sure he was too little to remember, but he enjoyed seeing that rainbow and hearing the story of Noah and God's promise to mankind.

To this day, I think of my precious grandson, Wyatt, every time I'm blessed to see a rainbow. I thank God for the precious times we've shared. I am reminded of how God made the rainbow as the sign of His promise. In His mercy, He has given mankind another chance. He sent Jesus. God made a way for our salvation and to form a relationship with Him. That old wooden cross was like that wooden door on the ark. By trusting what Jesus did there on that cross, we are safe from destruction, just like Noah and all those who went through that door. What mercy! What grace! What love!

Yes, I still think of Wyatt every time I see a rainbow and thank God for the precious time we've shared here on this Earth. But now, I also thank God for the eternity we will share. You see, God answered this grandma's prayers when Wyatt accepted Jesus and His mercy and grace. Jesus—the Door to eternal life!

The Good Shepherd

"Even if I walk through a very dark valley, I will not be afraid because You are with me. Your rod and your walking stick comfort me." Psalm 23: 4 (NCV)

My daddy was a very special man. He taught me so much about Jesus from his sermons at our little country church on Pleasant Ridge, and from the Bible stories he told my sister and me as we sat on his lap as little girls. But even more than that, he showed us who Jesus was by his actions.

One summer, one of my older brothers, Milton, was in the hospital to have surgery on his left hand. I remember one Saturday morning, my other older brother, Maurice, came to pick up my parents to go to the hospital and visit Milton. The old truck must not have been running, because Daddy told us to get ready to "hike on over" to Mr. and Mrs. Iberg's house. So, right after breakfast, Mike, Millie, and I followed Daddy through the woods to the neighbor's house. I remember how he made me feel safe. You see, Daddy would tell us kids to be careful where we stepped because of the snakes, but he always had a walking stick to use on anything that would harm us. We followed close behind him and knew we would be safe.

Daddy's gone now, but the Jesus he showed me has led me safely through many dark valleys, and I know He'll lead me safely home.

Bubbles, Sidewalk Chalk, and Love

> *"The Word became a human and lived among us. We saw His glory—the glory that belongs to the only Son of the Father—and He was full of grace and truth."* John 1: 14 (NCV)

Sometimes you are in the right place at the right time to witness something precious. One such day was in the first summer of little baby Khol's life. My daughter was caring for Khol, and my job (if you can call it that) was to play with big brother Carson and big sister Rayne. Outside is always the best place to be when you are two years old, so as soon as the last morsel of breakfast was swallowed, out the door we went with bubbles in hand. I can't say who had the most fun with those little bottles of magic. Was it Carson and Rayne, squealing with sheer delight as they chased the bubbles, jumping as high as they could to catch them? Or was it MaMa, laughing with sheer delight as I beheld life at its best? But, as beautiful as that memory was, one more topped it that day.

Next on our list was coloring with sidewalk chalk. Carson was content with drawing squiggly lines and circles, but Rayne wanted me to draw something for her. "MaMa, draw me. Draw Carson. Draw mommy. Draw daddy. Draw baby Khol. Ahh, Baby Khol! I kiss Baby Khol." Then, this precious little girl laid down, kissed Baby Khol's chalk face, and put her cheek on his. I will never forget that beautiful chalk-covered face. She had such love for her baby brother that she included him in her play.

I'm reminded of a Big Brother who came down from Heaven to show us His love. He includes us in His life not just for one beautiful, sunny afternoon, but forever and ever. Oh, what love!

Sowing Seeds

"But the Lord answered her, "Martha, Martha, you are worried and upset about many things. Only one thing is important. Mary has chosen the better thing, and it will never be taken from her." Luke 10: 41-42 (NCV)

My husband had a job to do. My son-in-law David said he'd be glad to help, and two-and-a-half-year-old twins, Carson and Rayne, were eager to help as well. Dan brought a bag of grass seed to the front yard, and the team set to work. The twins each retrieved handfuls of seeds and scattered them on the bare soil. Eventually, little Rayne couldn't help but notice the pretty roses nearby. Her grandpa watched her smell them, touch them, then pick at them. The petals came off easily. She was soon pulling handfuls of petals off—pink, peach, and red. Carson thought that looked like great fun, so he followed Rayne's lead—scattering beautiful rose petal "seeds" all over the front yard.

Oh, to look at life so simply, and with such childlike wonder! Have you lost it? Are you a Martha, always busy with taking care of a home and never taking time to sit with Jesus? Or are you a Mary, sitting at Jesus' feet, listening, learning, doing the better thing? The pre-resurrection Peter, always quick to act? Or a John the Beloved, always quick to listen, then act? Sometimes we need to be busy working or standing against the enemy; but, how much more could we accomplish for the Kingdom, if we spent time in His presence in awe of Him. What sheer joy we miss!

Won't you spend time today In His presence, and then join Him in His work?

Ready, Set, Go!

"We have around us many people whose lives tell us what faith means. So let us run the race that is before us and never give up. We should remove from our lives anything that would get in the way and the sin that so easily holds us back." Hebrews 12:1 (NCV)

When our two oldest grandsons were small, we were blessed to have their family stay with us for several months. Every night, after baths were done, Wyatt (five) and Mason (three) would stand in the hallway, clad in pajamas, anxiously awaiting their grandpa's "Ready, set, go!" The race was on! Through the living room, around the dining room table, and back again to the hallway. All the time, cheers came from mommy, daddy, grandpa, and me. No matter how many times Mason came in last, he never quit. How could he lose with all those people cheering him on? Sometimes, even big brother, Wyatt, would slow down and cheer him on to victory!

What a beautiful picture of what encouragement can do for us, His children, as we run our race here on Earth. Hebrews is full of encouraging testimonies of God's mighty power to help. Abel, Enoch, Noah, Abraham, Isaac, Jacob, Moses' parents (yes, parents play an important part in God's plan for their children), Moses, Rahab (no matter what our past is), Gideon (no matter how brave we are).

Take time to read the rest of the names in the eleventh chapter of Hebrews. What an amazing God! Time after time He can be trusted to be there for us and give us what we need, when we need it, to be victorious. He wants us to be victorious!

There is hope, my friend! Just never quit running. He'll be right there with you, all the way to the finish line.

Words

"Pleasant words are like a honeycomb, making people happy and healthy:" Proverbs 16:24 (NCV)

Khol is a man of few words. Of course, he's only two years old. But he communicates very effectively. On my wonderful weekly visits to "Stewartland", he is always waiting at the front door, right behind big brother and sister. After hugs to welcome me, he gets a sad face and says, "PaPa, work. Daddy, work." His joy is not complete if we aren't all there to share the day. I know the feeling.

One day when my husband was there, Khol pointed to a little pile of dirt and grass on the patio. He said, "Carson did it." Then he shrugged his little shoulders, looked at us, and said, "It happens." Oh, to be like a sweet little child, and keep the small stuff, the small stuff.

But nothing is so sweet to me as when little Kohl looks up to me and says, "I wuv you, MaMa!" Enough said. Effective communication. Mission accomplished.

God spoke the world into being. He sent Jesus, the Living Word, to our world. Jesus communicated His love for all mankind on Calvary. He communicated hope when He rose from the grave. He communicates "I am here" through the beauty in nature. Effective communication, wouldn't you say?

Now, what about us? Are we effective communicators of His love, mercy, forgiveness, and encouragement? Jesus said of believers, "Out of his belly shall flow rivers of living water." (John 3:38. KJV). Is life "'flowing' through us? Or has it become stagnant? Do our words bring life-giving water? Or are they smelly, mosquito-infested swamps spreading discouragement? The Apostle Paul spoke time after time of encouraging each other.

I believe I'll take Khol's lead and say some pleasant words today. How about you?

He's Watching You

"If you will be calm and trust Him, you will be strong." Isaiah 30:15 (NCV)

"For He is our God; and we are the people of His pasture, and the sheep of His hand." Psalm 95: 7 (KJV)

"He who guards Israel never rests or sleeps." Psalm 121:4 (NCV)

"God even knows how many hairs are on your head." Matthew 10:30 (NCV)

The buck just stood there firmly. He looked tall and majestic. He was on guard, protecting the does behind him. Another buck had started walking toward the does, but when he saw the buck standing guard, he took off running. All the first buck did was stand there-feet planted firmly on the crest of the hill in the open field, watching his does graze. They would be able to eat in peace till they were satisfied. He would see to it they had all they needed to sustain them. They were his to protect.

Jesus stands strong and firm. He is always watching us, making sure we are safe and have everything to sustain us physically, spiritually, mentally, and emotionally. He never sleeps, He never slumbers. (Psalm 121:4). He is always vigilant. We are precious to Him. He watches us so close that He knows the very number of hairs on our heads. (Matthew 10:30). We need not fear.

    What are you facing today, just to survive? Remember, He is watching over you. Remember, His vantage point is Heaven—higher than the crest of the hill. He can see the whole picture. He knows your past, your present, and your future! May His peace flood your heart today as you picture Him there, right in the middle of your circumstances. He's got you covered!

Brotherly Love

"Let brotherly love continue." Hebrews 13:1 (KJV)

My granddaughter Izabelle Grace laid there in her mommy's arms. She was so peaceful, so trusting. She knew mommy would take perfect care of her. But the dry heat that kept the house warm during the winter had taken its toll on Izzy's lips. All the lotions and creams couldn't fix it. Izzy's delicate newborn skin was not cooperating.

Big brother Khol (now a big twenty months old) stood close by, listening as my daughter and I talked about what we could try next. He left quietly, then appeared from his mommy's bedroom. He tenderly handed her the lip balm he had retrieved from her drawer, saying, "Baby, baby", as he pointed to Izzy's lips. What a precious picture of brotherly love!

"Let brotherly love continue." Four simple words. Simple instructions, yet important instructions.

How many times have we, as adults, complicated His instructions with excuses or reasons why we shouldn't extend love to someone? We can get back on track. Our all-wise, all-knowing, all-loving Heavenly Father gave us more simple instructions to help us. John the Revelator wrote to the church at Ephesus in Revelation 2: 5, "So remember where you were before you fell. Change your hearts and do what you did at first." It's so simple. Look back to Calvary—where you were cleansed and made pure by His precious blood. He loved unconditionally. He forgave eternally. He showed mercy in abundance.

In what way is He saying to you today to "let brotherly love continue"? A simple act of kindness? A helping hand? A kind word to a weary soul? A meal? A ride? Forgiveness? He knows we are human. Remember, He was one of us. He knows what we can do. Yet, we know what He can do. He showed us on Calvary. "Let brotherly love continue."

Mama

"My child pay attention to my words; listen closely to what I say. Don't ever forget my words; keep them always in mind. They are the key to life for those who find them; they bring health to the whole body. Be careful what you think, because your thoughts run your life."
Proverbs 4: 20-23 (NCV)

Mama is one of the most beautiful words in the English language. Her given name was Emma Eliza Ellen McKenzie, but to me and my thirteen older siblings, she was always "Mama." Her beauty was captivating—both on the outside and the inside. Her long dark hair with silver highlights was always braided and pinned on the crown of her head like a crown. It's no wonder that I always thought of her as a queen. She was Daddy's queen and our queen—all fourteen of us kids! I don't believe we ever gave her all the honor due to our queen, but Daddy did. Mama told me that after the older kids came along, Daddy said, "Babe, don't worry about gettin' breakfast, I'll take care of it. You need to stay in bed and get your rest." (I didn't know until I went to school that everybody's daddy didn't make their breakfast!) Daddy also made sure us kids gave Mama due respect. Most of the time, it was easy to show respect, it's just what you did. But when we thought we knew more than Mama did and the sass started, look out! The sassy one was escorted to the peach tree to remove a switch, which was used to administer proper correction. As a small child, I managed to keep myself out of trouble most of the time, but I'll never forget one day when I was eleven years old. I felt much more educated, intelligent, and "in touch" with the world than my antiquated parents. Mama told me to stop doing something, and I responded as only a "worldly" eleven- year-old could. I don't know whether it was the smart aleck attitude or the curse word I said, but the back side of her hand connected to my smart mouth. I was in shock! But a curse word did not pass my lips after that. Wise, loving parents, wouldn't you say?

    The love and tenderness my Mama showed her children, grandchildren, and great-grandchildren came from a heart of pure gold. Although she didn't have a lot of money, Mama always made us feel special. A little dress made from flour sacks. Little doll dresses made from scraps of fabric and lace. Her special "harvest" birthday cake. Cooking each of our favorite meals, even after we had families of our own. She did all-day laundry day on Monday using a wringer-washer and clothesline dryer, yet we still came home from school to the wonderful aroma of her famous homemade buns and a big pot of navy beans and ham bone. She never took a summer vacation, that time was for breaking beans, making jelly, and making sure the cellar walls were lined with mason jars filled with fruit and vegetables to feed us through the winter. She made sure my older sisters (and their friends) had beautiful crepe paper rose covered hoops for the yearly May Fete dance at school. She handmade each of us a set of embroidered dish towels and pillowcases when we got married.

The list goes on, but I think you get the picture. Although she raised fourteen of us, she loved each of us as though we were her only child. After we were all gone from home, that heart of gold reached out to a young man she'd never met. I know his heart was touched with God's faithful love as he read letters from Mrs. Vickers every week there in his prison cell.

I couldn't finish without telling you about my earliest memories. I would sit on Mama's lap, helping her break beans, while she told me the stories of little David being used by God to defeat Goliath, and young Joseph who had big dreams. I knew that, although I was little, God had good plans for me. So, as a thirteen-year-old girl, I answered God's call on my life to minister to precious young women who needed Jesus to "pick up the broken pieces" and heal their broken lives. Then, after high school graduation I went to Bible college, followed by the Continental Trailways bus ride to the Muskegon, Michigan, Teen Challenge Women's Unit. Mama was so proud of me and happy for me. But her favorite "Maidie" story made her eyes sparkle as she shared how I ran to the altar and gave my heart to Jesus. She knew that was the day she had prayed for, the day that would make all the difference in my life.

Thank you, Lord, for Mama. For her love, and most of all, for her prayers!

Clean Windows

"The eyes of your understanding being enlightened; that ye may know what is the hope of His calling, and what the riches of the glory of His inheritance of the saints. And what is the exceeding greatness of His power to us-ward who believe, according to the working of His mighty power, which He wrought in Christ, when He raised Him from the dead, and set Him at His own right hand in the heavenly places." Ephesians 1: 18-20 (KJV)

Winter can wreak havoc on a person. The older I get, the more aches and pains I experience when it's cold. The lack of sunshine impacts my outlook on life. The windows in my house get dirty and make it difficult to see the beauty God gave us. But last week God gave us a beautiful, warm, sunny day. It was perfect for washing windows! It made such a difference! Today, as I look out those same windows, in the middle of winter, I am enjoying the beautiful blue sky, fluffy white clouds, green cedar trees, and horses grazing in the pasture. Before the "window washing" I avoided looking out, for all I could focus on was the dirt that needed to be removed.

God is so good! He loves us so much! He wants to "clean our windows." He doesn't want us looking ***at*** dirty windows, but He wants us to look ***through*** clean windows.

They say that the eyes are the window to the soul. In Genesis 16: 13, Hagar called God "The Living One who sees me." He sees us and wants us to see Him! He doesn't want anything, not even a little "dirt" to obscure our view of Him. The key passage was a prayer that God put in Paul's heart to write to the church at Ephesus. It still is God's heart for us today. Just as my windows needed cleaning to see His nature, my soul needs constant cleaning to see Him clearer each day.

Thank God for a beautiful, warm day in the middle of my "winter." But I thank Him even more so that I can come to Him every day for the "washing of water by the Word," as in Ephesians 5:26. Or, "the commandment of the Lord is pure, enlightening the eyes," as in Psalm 19: 8. What a wise and wonderful God we serve!

Princesses

"Behold what manner of love the Father hath bestowed upon us, that we should be called the sons (children) of God." 1 John 3: (KJV)

"The Spirit itself beareth witness with our spirit, that we are the children of God; and if children, then heirs; heirs of God, and joint-heirs with Christ; if so be that we suffer with Him, that we may be also glorified together. For I reckon that the sufferings of this present time are not worthy to be compared with the glory which shall be revealed in us." Romans 8: 16-18 (KJV)

"And we know that all things work together for good to them that love God, to them who are the called according to His purpose." Romans 8:28 (KJV)

Four-year-old Rayne knows who she is; she is a princess. She has the dresses to prove it! But a few weeks ago, this little blonde-haired, blue-eyed girl wasn't looking so much like a princess, but more like an orphan. The princess dresses were torn and spotted. One looked as though it was beyond repair. MaMa tried to mend them. The first two didn't take too long to restore, but the last one took several hours. I had to sort through layers of chiffon, satin, and velveteen, gather each layer; then, sew them all together. Rayne was one happy little girl when she was once again "Princess Anna!"

Do you know that you are His precious child? If you have received Him in your heart, you are precious to Him. Do you know what that makes you? A child of a king is a prince or princess. We are children of the King of Kings! Hallelujah! But even His precious children get bruised, their hearts get broken, and misunderstandings happen. Jesus is there to mend us and even make us stronger because of it. He knows the pattern. He can put us back together.

Read the rest of Romans 8. You'll see you're in good hands, and nothing, yes, nothing, can separate you from His love.

Sunsets

"We have troubles all around us, but we are not defeated. We do not know what to do, but we do not give up the hope of living. We are persecuted, but God does not leave us. We are hurt sometimes, but we are not destroyed." 2 Corinthians 4: 8-9 (NCV)

"We have small troubles for a while now, but they are helping us gain an eternal glory that is much greater than the troubles. We set our eyes not on what we see but on what we cannot see. What we see will last only a short time, but what we cannot see will last forever." 2 Corinthians 4: 17-18 (NCV)

Sunsets are God's daily masterpieces. You know the ones I'm talking about- they take your breath away! I've been blessed to see them over mountains and over the ocean. But none have been more beautiful than the ones I've seen right out my backdoor; sunsets I've been blessed to share with my precious grandson, Mason.

As a young person, I remember trying to catch the beauty of God's handiwork on camera. The sunsets I caught on camera over Lake Michigan and Lake Lorraine were still no match for the ones I shared with little Mason. There seems to be a renewed sense of awe and wonder of our Creator as we see it on the face of a child. Our God is truly awesome! He loves us so much to show us such beauty!

One thing I have observed about sunsets is that the most magnificent ones are painted on clouds. The darker the clouds, the deeper, more intense, the colors are. Do you think He could be showing us more of who He is through the "dark clouds" of our lives? Let's let Him paint, so others will be drawn to His beauty. May His beauty in our life take someone's breath away, so He can breathe new life into them. What an awesome, wise, wonderful God we serve!

And, yes, still to this day, I think of Mason whenever I see a beautiful sunset. And I thank God for all the time we've been blessed to share on this Earth. Then I thank God for the eternity we will share. No more sunsets are needed to see His beauty. The Son will never leave. There will never be a night. Yes, this grandma's prayers were answered. Mason accepted the Son and He lights his life.

Our Great Big Protector

"The angel of the Lord encampeth round about them that fear Him, and delivereth them."
Psalm 34: 7 (KJV)

It was a dark and gloomy Sunday in May of 1989. My sister, Millie, her husband, Ron, and their three children were making the long trek north to Illinois to grieve the passing of our brother, Muerl. Ron requested prayer from his church family for travelling mercies. One little old lady prayed that God would send His angel to protect them on their journey.

Water remained on the road from the hard rain. Ron slowed down to avoid the deluge coming from the semi just ahead. Keeping a safe distance back, they travelled on. He saw a car approaching quickly from behind. The car flew past Ron's car, then hydroplaned in front of Ron. Ron said it all happened so fast, he just remembered slamming on the brakes and trying to stay on the road, to no avail. The car went backwards down an embankment about fifty feet from the highway. It stopped two feet shy of going into a four-foot drainage ditch, which would have flipped the car.

When the police arrived, one officer took Millie, Mindy, and Ray to town to get a tow truck. The other policeman stayed with Ron and 10-year-old Wil. The policeman said to Ron, "I don't know what stopped you from turning over." Wil looked at his dad and said, "But Dad, didn't you see him?"

"See who, son?"

"The angel. He disappeared when we stopped!"

Ron asked Wil what the angel looked like. With wide-eyes, Wil said, "He was about seven feet tall and dressed in white!"

Wow! God is always there to protect us.

Why did God let the car go into a tailspin in the first place? I don't know all the answers. But I do know that Ron, Millie, Mindy, Ray, and Wil were safe in His arms. And so are you and me.

And don't forget: God still answers the prayers of little old ladies.

Prayer Warriors

> *"Confess your sins to each other and pray for each other so God can heal you. When a believing person prays, great things happen. Elijah was a human being just like us. He prayed that it would not rain, and it did not rain on the land for three and a half years! Then Elijah prayed again, and the rain came down from the sky, and the land produced crops again."* James 5:16-18 (NCV)

We all know someone we would consider a prayer warrior. The first one I remember was my daddy. When one of the kids were sick, he would gently touch our foreheads with a dab of olive oil, pray like he was talking to his Best Friend, and then healing came (sometimes immediate—sometimes through a doctor's care). We knew he loved us, and so did his Best Friend, Jesus.

Although my mama didn't know I was listening, many nights I could hear her praying as she lay on her bed. She would call each of her children's names out in prayer—all fourteen of us. One by one, I saw those prayers answered. One prayer was answered only days before my brother passed away. And my oldest brother accepted Jesus when he was eighty years old. He went to be with the Lord when he was eighty-one. Although Mama was already with Jesus, her prayers were answered.

Then, there was Betty. She took prayer requests personally, like it was happening to her family. And it was! Her Christian brothers and sisters knew they could count on Betty to pray. When Betty led prayer at church, you felt the power of God. And you knew it didn't stop there, because Betty would ask you later how things were going with whatever situation it was. She was still praying, and you knew good things were going to happen.

I think of my sister, along with countless other "little old ladies" in churches all over. They take the prayer list on the bulletin seriously. No matter how long it takes, every request is lifted before God's throne.

My dear friends don't just talk about troubles and trials, they pray! Many a phone conversation has ended with a prayer that made me sense the very presence of God, knowing that someone lifted me up before God's throne. And I knew something good was going to happen. God was on the move because of a believer's prayer.

Finally, there are my grandchildren. How precious to hear their message on the answering machine saying, "We're praying for you, MaMa!" "We're praying for you, PaPa!" Their mommy taught them when they were young about Who is in control.

Have you seen yourself in any of these examples? Are you a believer? God can use you to make great things happen!

The Control Button

"Control yourselves and be careful! The devil, your enemy, goes around like a roaring lion looking for someone to eat. Refuse to give in to him, by standing strong in your faith. You know that your Christian family all over the world is having the same kinds of suffering." I Peter 5:8-9 (NCV)

God blessed me with much more than I deserve when He allowed me to be the youngest of fourteen children to be born to wonderful Christian parents. Yes, I was the baby of the family, and I was spoiled rotten by my mama, daddy, and all those older brothers and sisters. Life was good! Life was fun! But life was also, well, life! As the youngest, I had many examples of what to do and what not to do, to avoid the dreaded switch. My mama had to deal with three teenage girls at one time. Imagine the swift mood-swings with all those raging hormones. Then, she had my red-headed brother with the proverbial temper to deal with. Finally, she had my sister Millie and me to deal with. We weren't always cute. We made big messes. We bickered back and forth. And I was always tattling. It's a wonder they let me see eleven years old!

Ah, yes, eleven years old!? Remember the incident I wrote about in a previous devotion, titled "Mama", about a day when I was helping her in the kitchen? I was certainly out of control that day!

Through the years, and in all these circumstances, I remember one phrase coming from my mama's lips frequently: "Git a hold of yourself!" Oh, how she tried to teach us to "pass up the panic button" and go for peace. She knew that being "out of control" meant being "under the control" of the devil. Bad things would happen!

Throughout my adult life, I've had many times when things didn't go the way I wanted, or even the way they should have. Too many times I've lost control and hit the panic button. But, when I finally got control of myself, I gave control back to the Holy Spirit and trusted Him to do what was best. He always brought good things out of it. He can always be trusted.

Are you facing a situation today? God's Word says you can do all things through Christ who gives you strength. Pass up the panic button and go for peace. And remember we're all in this together—I pray for you; you pray for me.

He Took His Flight Also

"Precious in the sight of the Lord is the death of his saints." Psalms 116:15 (KJV)

When I was a teenager, I babysat my sister, Marilyn Kay's, two small children quite often when she went to visit her husband, Wayne, as he lay in the hospital in the final stage of cancer. I will never forget the day of my sister's last trip there. Wayne's brother John had just pulled out of the driveway after telling me that my sister would be home a little later, she had to make arrangements. I was stunned. The news was expected, but not so soon.

Little Wayne's cry made me snap back into reality and brought an uncontrollable flood of tears to my own eyes. I picked up little Wayne, who was named after his father, held him close, and then fed him his bottle. Concerned two-and-a-half-year-old Tina put her little hand on my arm and said, "Why cryin', Maida?" How could I tell her that her daddy was gone? Tina's tears beckoned an answer. I moved over and let Tina climb up into the big armchair in the corner of the small living room with Wayne and me.

I tried to explain to Tina what had happened. "Today, Jesus took your daddy home to be with Him. Jesus let daddy live with you and mommy and little Wayne for a while, but He wants daddy to live in Heaven with Him now." As the lump in my throat grew larger, I continued.

"So, you won't see daddy again for a long time, not until Jesus takes you to live in His house, too."

Tina sat thinking. I remembered the week before Christmas when my mom had come from Wayne's hospital room, her eyes filled with tears. "He's got cancer—only six more months, only six more months," she said. It was true. He gradually got worse and worse. I remembered the last Sunday he was able to go to the little country church where my daddy pastored. Even though pain shot through his frail body, he was able to sing his favorite song, "Mansion Over the Hilltop" from the depths of his cleansed heart.

The sound of Tina's voice broke into my thoughts and brought me back to reality. All she said was, "Outside, Maida." Her little forehead was covered with beads of perspiration from the August heat. I put the sleeping baby in his crib and took Tina's hand and led her out onto the back porch. Tina let go of my hand and pointed to a bird that had risen from the ground and was flying high in the sky. She turned to me, smiled, and said, "Daddy."

Even though my eyes were filled with tears of sorrow, my heart was filled with peace. I knew, and Tina knew, that Wayne's soul was taking its flight also, rising into Heaven.

Who do you Prefer?

> *"Be kindly affectioned one to another with brotherly love; in honor preferring one another."*
> *Romans 12: 10 (KJV)*

It was a hot summer day, but the trip to Wal-Mart was inevitable. Mommy (my daughter Emma) was organized, and everything would work like a well-oiled machine if everyone followed instructions. Carson and Rayne knew the procedure. They should pick up their water bottle and snack cup, go to the van, get in their car seats, and wait for Mommy to buckle them in. Then, they would head down the road for another adventure. However, Rayne forgot step number one. Mommy noticed as she was settling Khol in and reminded Rayne. Rayne looked over at Carson, and without a word spoken, Carson put his drink and snack down, went back in the house, and returned with Rayne's drink and snack. What a kind brother!

Fast forward two years. It was an unseasonably warm winter day. Carson, Rayne, and Khol came back in the house hungry and thirsty! They had played hard all morning and needed to refuel for a little more outside play before naptime. Everyone was in the kitchen making lunch and getting drinks. Everyone except Carson and Isabelle Grace. What I saw around the corner melted my heart. Carson was sweetly talking to his baby sister and kissing her gently on the forehead. In the middle of all the hubbub, he chose to include his baby sister. I couldn't help but think of Psalms 133:1 that says, "How good and how pleasant it is for brethren to dwell together in unity!"

Carson demonstrates two beautiful pictures of "kind affection" and "brotherly love." What might this look like in your life today? A smile? An encouraging word? A listening ear? Going out of your comfort zone to offer grace or mercy? All are simple things we all can do, but we never know what kind of difference it can make in someone else's life. Keep up the good work!

Life Giving Water

"But whosoever drinketh the water that I shall give him shall never thirst; but the water that I shall give him shall be in him a well of water springing up into everlasting life." John 4:14 (KJV)

One afternoon when I was in Stewartland, it was raining outside. What fun could that be for four little ones? It was time to create something beautiful indoors. Let's see. Did we have everything we needed? Paper, paint brushes, watercolors, little jars of water. Now the fun began! What would it be – a green dinosaur, pink piggies, blue butterflies on orange flowers, or a yellow sun over a blue-green pond with a fishing pole in the hand of a little red-headed fisherman? So many colors. So many works of art were made. Four proud painters. One proud grandma with beautiful works of art for her refrigerator.

But when they were smaller, they were so happy to just dip their little brushes in water. And when the water hit that magically prepared paper – WOW! All kinds of beautiful, colorful objects appeared like magic! In both cases, water was the key ingredient to creating beauty.

The woman at the well needed that key ingredient – WATER. Not just any water – she needed life-giving water. Then she met Jesus, the only One who could give that water. And when she received it, it was like going from black and white to full, glorious color! She had changed! She couldn't contain her newfound life. She left her water pots and ran into town to tell everyone about the One that could do the same for them. Her testimony brought many to Jesus. They wanted what she had!

So, where are you today? Have you been to the well? Or are you still thirsty? Jesus, the only One who can give that living water, is waiting. He is waiting for you and me. He is inviting you and me. **Come! Come Drink! Come Live Forever!**

Let's all let that bubbling spring of everlasting life color our lives today!

Leftovers

"They all ate and were satisfied, and what was leftover was gathered up, filling twelve baskets."
Luke 9:17 (NCV)

To some people, leftovers are a bad thing. But at our house, leftovers mean we can work a little longer in the garden, run one more errand, read one more chapter, visit a friend for a little longer, or play one more game. Leftovers can mean a smorgasbord supper, one pot wonder, or, on a cold winter evening, a great pot of soup to warm you from the inside out. And left-over chocolate chip cookies are quite a treat for the next day.

But today I am thinking of another kind of leftover. The kind of leftovers from a day with our daughter, son-in-law, and their four precious children.

As I folded beach towels, my heart was reminded of the laughter of the four little ones as they jumped in the pool and splashed each other in the warm sun. As I walked by the coffee table, I saw two tiny dolls. I smiled, remembering how much imagination those two little girls must have to enjoy a respite from the summer heat by constructing dolls. On the end table I spotted Legos. I smiled, remembering the skills those two little boys must have to build all kinds of things. The little stool was left in front of the bathroom sink. I smiled, remembering those dirty little hands that needed washing because they could all run and play and climb on the old tractor tires. And I remembered the joy on four-year-old Izzy's face as she climbed all the way across the monkey bars. And the sweet handprints on the door glass reminded me that they were all here to share a day with Grandpa and Grandma. The "leftovers" made me smile.

Just as the 5000 stayed all day listening to Jesus and were satisfied with the "bread" that He gave them, I am satisfied with Him in my heart. No one can satisfy our hungering hearts like Him. And I find that the longer I know him, the more "leftovers" he blesses me with.

Friend, have you "tasted and seen that the Lord is good?" What kind of leftovers has he blessed you with? I venture to say that your baskets are full, too!

Enjoy! Enjoy!

Acknowledgements

To my heavenly Father for His endless love, Jesus Christ our Lord for His grace, and the Holy Spirit for His comfort and leading in my life.

To my mama and daddy for showing me who Jesus is and leading me to Him.

To my sisters for all their encouragement to keep writing and sharing.

To Kara, Barb, Holly, and Roni. May God bless you. Without your encouragement, patience, and expertise, this book would still be just a file on my computer.

To my prayer team. Many of you are mentioned by name in these devotions. Without your prayers and nudges, this finished work would not exist.

To my grandchildren—Wyatt, Mason, Carson, Rayne, Khol, and Izzy—for giving me so many precious lessons. What joy you all bring to my life!

To my daughters. Rebecca, for all the sweet memories of laughter around the table. You always had a way with a story that could keep us laughing. Emma, for always seeing the best in everyone. What an encourager! Thank you for believing in my mission and me.

And finally, to my Dan for loving me and believing in me and the work God gave me to do. You never let me give up. You have always had such an unselfish, giving heart. God blessed me so when He brought you into my life. Thank you for sharing my journey. I love you.

CPSIA information can be obtained
at www.ICGtesting.com
Printed in the USA
JSHW042151070723
44350JS00003B/4